ST. LOUIS
CARDINALS

by Marty Gitlin

SportsZone

An Imprint of Abdo Publishing
www.abdopublishing.com

www.abdopublishing.com

Published by Abdo Publishing, a division of ABDO, PO Box 398166, Minneapolis, Minnesota 55439. Copyright © 2015 by Abdo Consulting Group, Inc. International copyrights reserved in all countries. No part of this book may be reproduced in any form without written permission from the publisher. SportsZone™ is a trademark and logo of Abdo Publishing.

Printed in the United States of America, North Mankato, Minnesota
052014
092014

Editor: Chrös McDougall
Copy Editor: Nicholas Cafarelli
Interior Design and Production: Carol Castro
Cover Design: Craig Hinton

Photo Credits: Tom DiPace/AP Images, cover; AP Images, 1, 4, 7, 9, 13, 15, 17, 18, 23, 24, 29, 33, 42, 43 (top), 44; George Grantham Bain Collection/Library of Congress, 10; Harry Hall/AP Images, 21; Diamond Images/Contributor/Getty Images, 26, 43 (middle); James A Finley/AP Images, 30; Gary Dineen/AP Images, 34; Al Behrman/AP Images, 37; Morry Gash/AP Images, 38; Bill Boyce/AP Images, 41, 43 (bottom); Tom Gannam/AP Images, 47

Library of Congress Control Number: 2014933060
Cataloging-in-Publication Data
Gitlin, Marty.
  St. Louis Cardinals / by Marty Gitlin.
     p. cm. — (Inside MLB)
  Includes bibliographical references and index.
  ISBN 978-1-62403-482-4
  1. St. Louis Cardinals (Baseball team)—History—Juvenile literature. I. Title.
  GV875.S74G47 2015
  796.357'640977866—dc23
                              2014933060

TABLE OF CONTENTS

CHAPTER 1

THE GREAT ESCAPE

The St. Louis Cardinals had reason to feel confident as summer turned into fall in 1964. They had just won three straight games against the Philadelphia Phillies. Now the New York Mets were coming to town. The 1964 Mets were one of the worst teams in the history of baseball.

The National League (NL) pennant race had become a mad scramble with one weekend remaining in the regular season. The Cardinals, the Phillies, the Cincinnati Reds, and the San Francisco Giants all remained in contention. But most people figured the Cardinals would easily beat the Mets and go on to win the title.

They figured wrong. The Mets had nothing to play for but pride and a chance to ruin the Cardinals' season. They set out to do just that. The Mets won the first two games of the series. One was a 15–5 embarrassment

Cardinals ace Bob Gibson pitches in the 1964 World Series. He won two of his three starts and struck out 31 batters in 27 innings.

in which the Cardinals committed five errors. The Cardinals were playing their worst baseball when they needed to play their best.

The Cardinals could at least force a one-game playoff with the Reds if they beat the Mets that Sunday. A loss would send the Cardinals packing their bags for the off-season.

The Cardinals rose to the occasion this time. They had 14 hits in an 11–5 win at Sportsman's Park in St. Louis. They clinched the pennant when the Reds lost to the Phillies.

Orlando Magic

The Cardinals had talented first baseman/outfielder Orlando Cepeda for only three seasons, but they certainly got the most out of him in 1967. Cepeda batted .325 with 25 home runs and led the NL with 111 runs batted in (RBIs) that year. He also won the league's Most Valuable Player (MVP) Award while helping the Cardinals win the pennant.

A celebration ensued in the Cardinals' locker room following the game. The fans were excited as well. Some 3,000 people gathered under the stairway leading to the team clubhouse. They chanted for every player and for manager Johnny Keane to come out and take a bow, and they got their wish. But the job was not finished. The Cardinals still had the mighty New York Yankees to deal with in the World Series.

The American League (AL) champion Yankees did not intimidate the Cardinals. St. Louis featured some of the most talented players in baseball. Top three starting pitchers Bob Gibson, Curt Simmons, and Ray Sadecki had combined for 57 wins that season. Barney Schultz was one of the best relievers in the game. The offense was led by speedy outfielders Lou Brock and Curt

Cardinals catcher Tim McCarver scores on a double steal in Game 7 of the 1964 World Series. The Cardinals held off the Yankees 7–5 for the win.

Flood and slugging infielders Bill White and Ken Boyer. The team was among the top three in the NL in runs scored, hits, doubles, triples, and stolen bases.

And just as the pennant race came down to the final game, so did the World Series. A sellout crowd of 30,346 stuffed themselves into tiny Sportsman's Park to watch Game 7.

They left in joyful celebration as Boyer hit a double and a home run to lead the Cardinals to a 7–5 victory. Gibson pitched the game on just two days of rest. But he threw a complete game and struck out nine Yankees to give his team its first World Series title since 1946.

Gibson's performance earned him MVP honors in the Series. But the Cardinals' tired

MR. BUSCH

August A. Busch Jr. was the president of Anheuser-Busch, the largest beer brewing company in the United States. But the man who was known affectionately as "Gussie" was also the Cardinals' owner and president when they won the 1964, 1967, and 1982 World Series. He was instrumental in creating a championship baseball team.

Born in 1899, Busch purchased the team from Fred Saigh before the 1954 season. He eventually tired of the club's mediocre performances and set out to build a winner—and the new Busch Stadium, which was finished in 1966. In the World Series title year of 1967, the Cardinals surpassed 2 million in attendance for the first time in their history.

Busch handed over the reins of the brewery to his son in 1975, but remained team owner and presided over the team during its pennant runs of the 1980s. He died at age 90 in 1989.

ace nearly lost it in the ninth inning. The right-hander gave up two home runs as the Yankees pulled to within two runs. When Keane was asked why he left Gibson in the game, he answered with a supreme compliment: "I had a commitment to his heart."

Gibson's heart and brilliance on the mound continued to result in Cardinals titles. He returned from a broken leg in 1967 to help the Cardinals win another pennant. He earned three of the team's four victories in that World Series triumph. Gibson crafted one of the greatest Series performances in history against the upstart Boston Red Sox. He won all three of his starts with an incredible 1.00 earned run average (ERA).

Brock played very well against the Red Sox, too. He batted .414 with eight runs

Cardinals teammates, *from left*, Lou Brock, Julian Javier, and Bob Gibson celebrate after beating the Boston Red Sox in the 1967 World Series.

and seven stolen bases. But Gibson stole the show.

"[He was] invincible," Cardinals catcher Tim McCarver said when asked about Gibson's performance. "He was everywhere. He just dominated the Series."

Gibson dominated the 1968 Series, as well. Brock also performed brilliantly. But Gibson and Brock had little help from their teammates as the Cardinals lost to the Detroit Tigers. The era of St. Louis baseball greatness was over, but only temporarily. That is the way it has always been for the Cardinals, one of the premier franchises in American sports.

CHAPTER 2

CARDINALS TAKE FLIGHT

The St. Louis baseball team was used to success as a member of the American Association in the 1880s. The club had a winning record every year from 1883 to 1891. It won four consecutive titles in the middle of that stretch. So it came as a bit of a shock for the team, then called the St. Louis Browns, when they joined the National League in 1892 and became an immediate laughingstock.

The Browns went from bad to worse. As the new century approached, they posted records such as 39–92, 40–90, 29–102, and 39–111. When owner Chris Von der Ahe and his corporation declared bankruptcy, they were forced to sell the team to brothers Frank and Stanley Robison in 1899.

The team changed its name to the Cardinals in 1900, and it soon returned to its winning ways. But after two strong

Ed Konetchy starred for the Cardinals from 1907 to 1913. He led the NL with 38 doubles in 1911.

THE GREAT HORNSBY

Rogers Hornsby is considered one of the best hitters in baseball history. His .424 batting average in 1924 has never been topped. He hit .313 or better in 13 of the 14 years he had more than 400 at-bats. He led the NL in hitting seven times. Hornsby also topped the NL in runs five times, doubles and RBIs four times each, and triples twice. As baseball became more of a power game, he increased his home-run totals, too. He hit 42 home runs in 1922 and 39 in 1925. His .358 career batting average is second in major league history after Ty Cobb's .366.

Hornsby was known as a player who had a passion for the sport. "People ask me what I do in winter when there's no baseball," he said. "I'll tell you what I do. I stare out the window and wait for spring."

seasons, the Redbirds—as the team is sometimes called—began to fly south in the standings yet again. They had at least 90 losses in eight of nine years beginning in 1905. They did not finish closer than 13 games out of first place until 1921.

It was in that year the Cardinals emerged as one of the top teams in the NL. Team president Branch Rickey helped build the team through a strong farm system. Future Hall of Fame second baseman Rogers Hornsby, who served as a player-manager, guided them to victory. The Cardinals finished 87–66 and third in the NL. They would never again taste long-term failure.

Rogers Hornsby played for the Cardinals from 1915 until 1926 and in 1933. He was one of the top batters in baseball history and won six straight batting titles from 1920 to 1925.

Everything came together in 1926. The Cardinals surrounded Hornsby with talent such as first baseman Jim Bottomley and third baseman Les Bell that season. Those two players combined for 36 home runs and 220 RBIs. Hornsby added 93 RBIs while batting .317. Flint Rhem won 20 games to lead a balanced pitching staff. With an 89–65 record, the Cardinals won their first pennant.

The Cardinals faced the powerful New York Yankees in the World Series. It all came down to the last nerve-wracking moment. The Cardinals led 3–2 with two out in the ninth inning of the seventh and deciding game. Then Yankees legendary slugger Babe Ruth surprised everyone by trying to steal second base. Cardinals catcher Bob O'Farrell threw him out, ending the game and handing St. Louis the title.

The Yankees got revenge in 1928. They swept the Cardinals in four games to win the World Series. Hornsby had left the Cardinals after the 1926 season, but the team did not slow down. They returned to the Fall Classic against the Philadelphia Athletics in 1930 and 1931. The Cardinals lost in 1930 but won the 1931 World Series in seven games.

Players such as first baseman Ripper Collins, second baseman Frankie Frisch, and outfielders Chick Hafey and

Still Strong

The Chicago Cubs thought Grover Cleveland Alexander was washed up when they released him in 1926. But they were wrong. One of the best pitchers in baseball history could still get batters out. He even got the last seven Yankees out in Game 7 of the 1926 World Series to clinch the title for the Cardinals. He then won a combined 37 games for St. Louis in 1927 and 1928.

Dizzy Dean, *left*, and Daffy Dean, *right*, pose with former Cardinal Grover Cleveland Alexander at spring training in 1935.

Pepper Martin made the Cardinals one of the top batting teams in the NL. Along with the pitching trio of Bill Hallahan, Burleigh Grimes, and Paul Derringer, the Cardinals were an NL force.

But it was pitcher Dizzy Dean who transformed the Cardinals from just a great team into what many have called the most colorful team in baseball history. The right-hander had a southern drawl, a wide array of homespun expressions, and a great pitching arm. He burst onto the baseball scene by winning 18 games in 1932.

Dean won at least 20 games in each of the next four years. He had records of 30–7 in 1934 and 28–12 the following season.

The 1934 Cardinals were dubbed "The Gas House Gang" for their zany personalities and rough style of play. By that time, they had added more talented players. One was an outfielder named Joe "Ducky" Medwick. Dean's talented brother Paul had also been added to the roster. Medwick batted .319 with 110 runs and 106 RBIs that season. Paul Dean (who was nicknamed Daffy) won 19 games.

The Gas House Gang won the pennant on the final day of the regular season. Then they split the first six games of the World Series against the Detroit Tigers. When Dizzy Dean shut out the Tigers in Game 7, the Cardinals were again champions. The legend of the Gas House Gang had been born. And it was relived and remembered for generations thereafter.

"The Cardinals . . . were a colorful group of ballplayers, aggressive, brash, loudmouthed, uninhibited," wrote *Sports Illustrated* writer Robert Creamer in 1957. ". . . Dizzy Dean . . . would mock an opposing batter . . . defying [him] to hit and laughing at him when he failed. Pepper

Ups and Downs

Attendance for Cardinals games at Sportsman's Park rose dramatically as the team began to win in the 1920s. It spiked to an all-time high of 668,000 in the title year of 1926 and increased in each of the next two seasons. The Cardinals continued to draw well until 1932. But the Great Depression then took a tremendous toll on Americans, who could no longer afford to attend games. Attendance didn't rise significantly again until after World War II in 1946.

Cardinals hurler Dizzy Dean mows down the Detroit Tigers' batters in the 1934 World Series.

Martin would . . . try for an extra base, lose his race with the throw coming from the outfield and then turn defeat into victory with a crunching headfirst slide that sent dust, his opponent, and the ball flying in different directions.

". . . They were a tough team, a rowdy team. They were supremely confident, and fiercely competitive, and they had almost no respect for anything but victory."

The times and the Cardinals would change. But their usually successful quest for victory would remain a constant into the twenty-first century.

CHAPTER 3

THE "STAN THE MAN" ERA

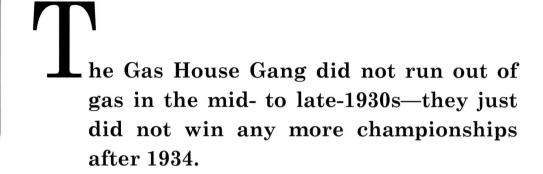

The Gas House Gang did not run out of gas in the mid- to late-1930s—they just did not win any more championships after 1934.

Dizzy Dean won 24 games in 1936. Joe Medwick continued to be one of the most productive players in baseball. He led the NL in batting average, home runs, and RBIs in 1937 to earn the rare Triple Crown. Young first baseman Johnny Mize emerged as a feared hitter. And outfielder Enos "Country" Slaughter hit 52 doubles to lead the NL in 1939.

A Golden Voice

Cardinals catcher Joe Garagiola became more famous after his playing career ended. Garagiola was never a full-time starter during his career in the late 1940s and early 1950s. He finished with a lifetime batting average of .257. But after he left the game, he became one of its most famous television personalities. He served as a broadcaster on the Major League Baseball (MLB) Game of the Week for many years and also hosted game shows.

Slugger Stan Musial played for the Cardinals from 1941 to 1944 and from 1946 until 1963. He was a three-time MVP and was runner-up four times.

Red of the Redbirds

St. Louis sluggers Stan Musial and Enos Slaughter got some offensive help from one player in the late 1940s and early 1950s. And that was second baseman and left fielder Red Schoendienst. Schoendienst continued to improve at the plate until he became a consistent .300 hitter late in his career. He led the NL with 43 doubles in 1950 and scored 80 or more runs in nine separate seasons. He went on to manage the Cardinals from 1965 to 1976 and guided the team to the World Series title in 1967. He also served as interim manager in both 1980 and 1990.

Two events in 1941 served as a prelude to more championships. The first was Billy Southworth's first full season as manager. The Cardinals won 97 games that season and finished a close second to the Brooklyn Dodgers in the NL. The second event was the debut of outfielder Stan "The Man" Musial. He took the league by storm by batting .426 in a brief September trial. By 1942, he was ready to become one of the greatest athletes in American sports.

And the Cardinals were ready to win another title. They won a team-record 106 games in 1942. They edged out the Dodgers for the pennant with a 21–4 record in September.

Mize had been traded to the Giants, but Musial and Slaughter paced the top-scoring offense in the league. Pitchers Mort Cooper and Johnny Beazley combined for a 43–13 record. Cooper was sensational, sporting a 22–7 record with a 1.78 ERA.

The Cardinals sputtered to a 7–4 loss in the World Series opener against the New York Yankees. But the Redbirds did have some consolation. They broke up a no-hitter by Yankees ace Red Ruffing in the eighth inning.

From left, Stan Musial, Enos Slaughter, and Terry Moore were among the NL's top batters in 1942.

"We'd thrown a scare into the Yankees," Cardinals pitcher Ernie White said. "And even though we'd lost, we couldn't wait to get back out on the field the next day."

White certainly pitched as if he could not wait to get back out on the field. After the Cardinals edged the Yankees in Game 2, White shut out the Yankees, 2–0, in Game 3. The Cardinals never let go of that lead.

An unlikely hero finalized the Cardinals' World Series

STAN MUSIAL

Stan Musial began his career as a promising pitcher until he suffered a shoulder injury while in the minor leagues. But the left-handed hitter could still slug the baseball. Musial led the NL in hits six times, doubles eight times, triples and runs five times each, and earned seven batting titles. He peaked in 1948, when he batted .376 and missed the Triple Crown by one home run. Musial made the NL All-Star team 24 times.

He remains one of the most beloved figures in St. Louis, not only for his legendary achievements on the field, but for his love for the city. His impact on the community was expressed by former Cardinals pitcher Dan Haren.

"The fans here understand what a guy like Stan Musial means to the game of baseball," Haren said. "They embrace him. They cherish him. He kind of has an aura around him. When he's walking through a room, everything stops."

win in Game 5. With the score tied 2–2, Whitey Kurowski slammed a game-winning home run off Ruffing.

During the early 1940s, MLB teams had lost many players who were called to fight in World War II. But the Redbirds remained strong. They buried the NL competition by winning 105 games in both 1943 and 1944.

They faced the Yankees again in the 1943 World Series. But the Yankees came out on top, winning four games to one.

The city of St. Louis drew greater excitement from the 1944 Fall Classic. It marked the first time that two teams from that town participated. The Cardinals played against the St. Louis Browns. Both teams shared Sportsman's Park. However, the Browns were

Sportsman's Park in St. Louis was the scene when the Cardinals and the Browns met in the 1944 World Series.

often considered second-class to the Cardinals in St. Louis. That did not change in the 1944 World Series. The Cardinals won in six games.

The Cardinals nearly won the pennant in 1945 despite losing their entire outfield to the war effort. But the return of Musial and Slaughter the

A Fine Fielder

Marty Marion did not scare too many pitchers with a bat in his hand, though he was a respectable hitter. But he is still considered one of the finest fielding shortstops in the history of the game. Marion was so good at that position that he won NL MVP honors in 1944 despite the fact that he batted only .267 with 50 runs and 63 RBIs that year.

Enos Slaughter slides into home plate to give the Cardinals the winning run of the 1946 World Series.

Happy Unveiling

After 47 years at Sportsman's Park, which was later renamed Busch Stadium, the Cardinals moved to a new, 50,000-seat Busch Stadium in 1966. The field was situated in the heart of downtown St. Louis. They played their first game at the new park on May 12 of that year and defeated the Atlanta Braves 4–3 on a game-winning single by Lou Brock in the 12th inning.

following season made them as strong as ever. Slaughter batted .365 and the pair combined for 233 RBIs. The Cardinals won 98 games and the NL pennant. Ace Howie Pollet had a record of 21–10 with a 2.10 ERA.

The 1946 World Series was among the most exciting in baseball history. The Cardinals and Boston Red Sox were tied at 3–3 in the eighth inning of Game 7. Then Slaughter singled and scored on a double by Harry Walker. Slaughter shocked Red Sox shortstop Johnny Pesky when he rounded third and tried to score on the play. Pesky's hesitation in throwing the ball gave Slaughter time to cross the plate.

The hero of the Series was Cardinals pitcher Harry "The Cat" Brecheen. He won three games—including the final game—by shutting down the Red Sox as a reliever.

Musial remained one of the top players in the game, but the Cardinals' run of championships was over. The Cardinals continued to contend into the early 1950s. But they simply could not find enough offensive help for Musial and Slaughter. The team slid into mediocrity as that decade progressed.

In 1963, a 42-year-old Musial played his last season. The Cardinals won 93 games and finished second in the NL. The talent on that team would blossom the next year, when Bob Gibson led them to the World Series title.

As the 1970s approached, Cardinals fans had plenty to cheer about again. But it would be a while before the team reached another Fall Classic.

Unhittable

Bob Gibson achieved arguably the greatest pitching season in history in 1968. In what was known as the "Year of the Pitcher" for the sensational performances on the mound, Gibson was the best of all. He compiled the lowest ERA ever at 1.12 while winning 22 games and striking out 268 batters. His dominance—and that of several other pitchers that season—motivated MLB to lower the mound in 1969 to give batters a better chance and to create more offense in the game.

CHAPTER 4

MEDIOCRITY TO GREATNESS

Bob Gibson was still an effective pitcher in 1971. But at age 35 he was closing in on the end of his career. The Cardinals appeared to have an ideal replacement. His name was Steve Carlton. The left-handed pitcher had been with the team since 1965. He blossomed in 1971, winning 20 games.

Carlton was expected to take over as the Cardinals' ace pitcher. But after the 1971 season, the team traded him to the Philadelphia Phillies for pitcher Rick Wise. Wise was a talented right-hander. He performed well in his two years for St. Louis. But Carlton blossomed into one of the best pitchers in baseball history. In 1972, he had an ERA of 1.97 and won 27 games for the lowly Phillies.

It took several years for the Cardinals to recover from the blunder. They had some talented batters like Lou Brock, Joe Torre, and Ted Simmons.

Cardinals hurler Bob Gibson won two Cy Young Awards, an MVP Award, and 251 games during his 17 seasons with the Cardinals.

But the team became inconsistent. Gibson retired after 17 seasons in 1975. The Cardinals had a solid pitching staff, but they lacked a true ace.

The Cardinals did not reach the postseason during the 1970s, but several players had standout seasons. Gibson had a 23–7 record in 1970. Torre led the NL in hitting in 1971 with a .363 average. He added 137 RBIs to win MVP honors that season. Brock stole a major league record 118 bases in 1974. In 1975, closer Al Hrabosky won the "Fireman of the Year" award. That award is presented to the top reliever in each league.

Starting pitcher John Denny had an NL-best ERA of 2.52 in 1976. Fellow pitcher Bob Forsch emerged to win 20 games in 1977. And young first baseman Keith Hernandez won the MVP Award in 1979 by batting .344 with a league-high 48 doubles.

It was not until June 9, 1980, that the Cardinals began to fly high again. That was the date Whitey Herzog was named manager. Two years later, the Cardinals were ready to contend. By that time they had other players to complement Hernandez. They included the outfield of speedy Willie McGee and Lonnie Smith, as well as George Hendrick, who led the team with 104 RBIs. The Cardinals had also acquired acrobatic shortstop Ozzie Smith from the San Diego Padres.

Starters Forsch and Joaquin Andujar led the pitching staff. Andujar blossomed in 1982 after experiencing little success in the major leagues. But the key hurler was closer Bruce Sutter. He used his signature sinking split-finger fastball to record 36 saves.

Keith Hernandez watches his home run take flight in a 1982 game. He played more than nine seasons in St. Louis and was the 1979 NL MVP.

The Cardinals swept past the Atlanta Braves in the NL Championship Series (NLCS). The high-powered Milwaukee Brewers awaited in the World Series. The 1982 Series had plenty of drama. The Redbirds were on the verge of defeat after losing three of the first five games. Then rookie pitcher John Stuper shut down the slugging Brewers, 13–1. It all came down to Game 7.

Fast Start

The 1982 Cardinals wasted little time taking control of the NL East Division. After losing three of their first four games, they embarked on a 12-game winning streak, which included sweeps of the Chicago Cubs, the Philadelphia Phillies, and the Pittsburgh Pirates.

Darrell Porter shakes hands with Cardinals' supporters during the team's 1982 World Series victory parade through downtown St. Louis.

Andujar proved to be the pitching hero of the Series. Despite an injury suffered in Game 3—when he took a line drive off his knee—he held the Brewers to three runs in seven innings in Game 7. Trailing 3–1 in the sixth, the Cardinals moved ahead on hits by Hernandez and George Hendrick. And in the last two innings,

Sutter did what he had done all year—clinched St. Louis victories. For the ninth time, the Cardinals were World Series champions. Only the New York Yankees had won more titles.

The unlikeliest hero was catcher Darrell Porter. He was a former Brewer who had been booed in St. Louis for his poor production. Porter redeemed himself in the World Series. He batted .286 with a home run and five RBIs while playing flawlessly behind the plate. He was named MVP in the Series.

More than 200,000 fans showed up in St. Louis for the victory parade. It was deemed the biggest celebration in the history of the city. Meanwhile, Herzog spoke about the ingredients needed to win a World Series title.

"The strange thing," he said, "is that when you have defense and speed and your pitchers don't walk batters and keep the ball in the ball park, you can win every game."

The Cardinals had indeed won the title in 1982 the way Herzog dreamed it up. They led the NL in fielding and stolen bases, and their pitchers gave up just three walks a game and 94 home runs all

"THE WIZARD OF OZ"

Ozzie Smith had a lifetime batting average of .262 and hit only 28 home runs during his 19-year career. But there was little doubt he would be voted into the Hall of Fame. After all, he was arguably the greatest defensive shortstop in baseball history. Smith won 13 Gold Gloves and was named to the NL All-Star team 15 times. His batting improved later in his career, when he consistently hit between .270 and .300. He was also one of the top base stealers in the game. But "The Wizard of Oz" will always be remembered for his great defense.

"The guys who get into the Hall of Fame are the guys who hit the ball out of the ballpark," he said. "I hope my going in will open the door for the other guys who have the ability to help their teams with defense."

year. Their speed and contact hitters had overcome the home-run sluggers from Milwaukee. But they were far from done.

Following their 1982 World Series title, the Cardinals won two more pennants in the next five years. Players such as second baseman Tommy Herr, Smith, and McGee remained throughout. But the Cardinals continued to thrive by continuing to add new talent. Slugging first baseman Jack Clark and speedy outfielder Vince Coleman improved the batting. Meanwhile, pitchers John Tudor and Danny Cox joined Andujar on the mound.

All the newcomers contributed greatly in 1985 as the Cardinals won 101 games and the pennant. The pitching trio combined for 60 wins. Tudor and Andujar each won 21 games. Clark hit 22 home runs. Coleman stole 110 bases and scored 107 runs. Herr racked up 110 RBIs despite hitting just eight home runs.

The Cardinals faced the cross-state rival Kansas City Royals in the World Series. The Cardinals appeared to have locked up a second World Series title in four years when Tudor shut out the Royals in Game 4. That gave the Cardinals a 3–1 series lead. But the Cardinals' bats went silent. They scored just two runs in the last three games and lost the Series.

A rash of injuries struck Herr, McGee, Tudor, and Clark in 1987. But the Redbirds still won the pennant and were again on the brink of a championship. They won three of the first five games of the World Series against the Minnesota Twins. But they lost the last two. The lack of an ace pitcher came back to haunt them in the World Series.

Ozzie Smith charges home as Royals catcher Jim Sundberg, *right*, awaits the throw during the 1985 World Series.

The Cardinals fell short in the World Series, but they pulled off an incredible feat just by getting there. The Cardinals had won the NL pennant with many backups playing major roles. Clark, their only power hitter, was even gone through the playoffs and World Series.

"If you're a St. Louis Cardinals fan, dab your eyes and give your team a big hand," wrote *Sports Illustrated*'s Steve Wulf. "The Cards almost overcame their lack of power with true grit and determination. 'It's amazing we got this far with a spring training B team out there,' said first baseman Jim Lindeman."

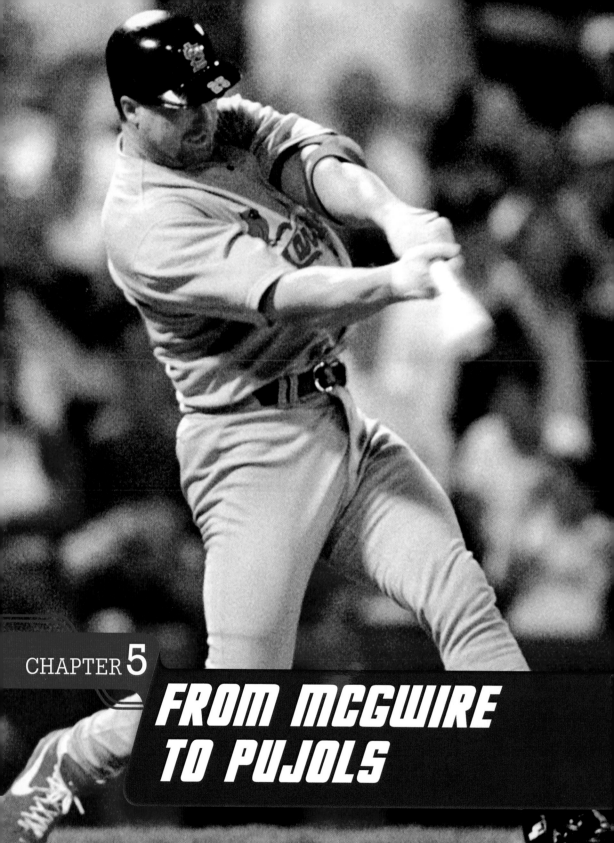

CHAPTER 5

FROM MCGWIRE
TO PUJOLS

The Cardinals were good in the 1990s—just not good enough to contend. They managed to win a division title in 1996. However, their problems putting away postseason opponents continued when they blew a 3–1 NLCS lead to the Atlanta Braves.

The Cardinals featured several great players during the decade. Among them were first baseman Pedro Guerrero and outfielders Ray Lankford and Brian Jordan. Starting pitchers Bob Tewksbury and Andy Benes and closer Lee Smith shined, as well.

But the greatest attention revolved around mammoth first baseman Mark McGwire. The Cardinals traded for McGwire in 1997 to bring much-needed power to their lineup. McGwire and Chicago Cubs outfielder Sammy Sosa both appeared on track to break the single-season

Mark McGwire proved to be the ultimate power hitter when he broke the single-season home run record in 1998. That record later came into question when he admitted to taking steroids.

home-run record early on in the 1998 season. The duo received much fanfare as they continued to blast home runs.

The previous record had been 61 home runs. McGwire ended the season with 70 and Sosa with 66. The attention they received helped MLB regain some popularity after a strike had shortened the 1994 season. Many fans who turned away in 1994 came back in 1998. McGwire's power-hitting dominance continued the next season when he hit 65 home runs.

McGwire's record was revered at the time. However, it was later revealed he was one of many players of his era who took performance-enhancing drugs such as steroids to increase their strength. Most feel all the home-run records set during the late 1990s into the 2000s were tainted. That period has become known as The Steroid Era.

Despite McGwire's home-run success, the Cardinals did not reach the playoffs in 1997, 1998, or 1999. But they quickly established themselves as a top team in the NL Central Division after that. The Cardinals reached the NLCS in 2000 but lost to the New York Mets. Their success continued throughout the decade. That was in large

Third baseman Scott Rolen's powerful bat and strong defense helped the Cardinals win the 2004 and 2006 NL pennants.

part due to the addition of a once-in-a-generation player.

Albert Pujols debuted in 2001. He immediately established himself as one of the finest hitters in baseball. He hit .329 with 37 home runs and 130 RBIs to be the 2001 NL Rookie of the Year. That type of production became standard for Pujols in the following years.

Along with outfielders Jim Edmonds and J. D. Drew, Pujols led the Cardinals to the playoffs as the wild card. But their season ended against the eventual champions, the Arizona Diamondbacks.

After retiring the final Tigers batter, Cardinals pitcher Adam Wainwright awaits his teammates to celebrate winning the 2006 World Series.

The Cardinals changed their attack from one featuring singles hitters and stolen bases to one boasting tremendous power. Pujols received protection in the lineup from the likes of outfielder Edmonds and third baseman Scott Rolen. Edmonds hit 39 home runs or more three times between 2000 and 2004. Shortstop Edgar Renteria also provided run production. Meanwhile, the Redbirds received excellent pitching from starters Darryl Kile, Matt Morris, Chris Carpenter, and closer Jason Isringhausen.

The Cardinals returned to the playoffs in 2002 but lost to the San Francisco Giants in the NLCS. After missing the 2003 playoffs, the Cardinals had an MLB-best 105 wins in 2004. They got all the way to the World Series that season. However, they ran into a Boston Red Sox team in the midst of a dream postseason and were swept in four games.

The Cardinals showed their consistency again in 2005, but again fell short of the World Series title. They lost to the Houston Astros in the NLCS.

In 2006, the Cardinals moved into a new Busch Stadium in downtown St. Louis. But after many successful seasons, it appeared as if the team was fading back into mediocrity that season. The Cardinals barely reached the playoffs after finishing 83–78 and winning a weak NL Central Division.

They finally hit their stride in the postseason. The Cardinals beat the San Diego Padres and the Mets in the playoffs. That set up a World Series showdown against the upstart Detroit Tigers.

The teams traded victories in the first two games. Then Carpenter and closer Braden Looper shut out the Tigers in Game 3. The Cardinals also won the next two games before their own fans at Busch Stadium to win their first World Series title since 1982.

"This is the most beautiful feeling in the world," Pujols said after his team had clinched the title. "These are the greatest fans in baseball. Hopefully, we don't have to wait another 24 years to do this again."

The Cardinals finished 78–84 in 2007. It was their only losing season between 2000 and 2010. Renteria had left after the 2004 season. Rolen and Edmonds each left after the 2007 season. But behind Pujols, Carpenter, and a new cast, the Cardinals remained a solid team.

Their 2008 record of 86–76 was good for only fourth that season. The Cardinals traded for outfielder Matt Holliday during the 2009 season. He batted .353 with 13 home runs and 55 RBIs in only 235 at–bats to help the Cardinals win the NL Central and return to the

postseason. However, the Los Angeles Dodgers swept them in the first round.

The Cardinals came back and finished 86–76 in 2010. However, their record was only good for second in the division, leaving them out of the postseason.

The Cardinals came back strong in 2011, winning the division to return to the postseason. They easily won the NLCS to advance to the World Series. In Game 7, they clinched the Series for their eleventh world championship.

Under new manager Mike Matheny in 2012, the Cardinals went on to win the division but lost the NLCS to the San Francisco Giants.

The next season was strong for the Cardinals. They advanced to the World Series, where the Boston Red Sox defeated them in Game 6. That

One-Two Punch

The Cardinals have had several great pitching tandems over the years, but arguably the top performances from two pitchers in one season occurred in 2009. During that year, Adam Wainwright and Chris Carpenter performed as well as anyone in the game. Wainwright led the NL with 19 victories and boasted a 2.63 ERA. Carpenter won 17 of 21 decisions with an NL-best 2.24 ERA.

Albert Pujols blasts a home run in a 2008 game. Pujols has consistently been one of the top hitters in the NL since debuting in 2001.

season, the Cardinals led the league in runs scored and ended with a strong roster.

The Cardinals have been consistently among the better teams. As the club has proven time and again, the Cardinals are always on the brink of winning another championship.

TIMELINE

1892	The St. Louis Browns join the NL after the American Association folds.
1914	Miller Huggins guides the Cardinals to an 81–72 record in his second season as manager.
1924	Rogers Hornsby sets a major league record that still stands with a .424 batting average.
1926	The Cardinals secure their first World Series title on October 10 with a 3–2 win over the New York Yankees.
1931	The Cardinals clinch their second World Series championship on October 10 with a 4–2 defeat of the Philadelphia Athletics in Game 7.
1934	The colorful "Gas House Gang" secures a World Series crown on October 9 by shutting out the Detroit Tigers, 11–0.
1937	Joe "Ducky" Medwick wins the NL Triple Crown with a .374 batting average, 31 home runs, and 154 RBIs.
1941	Stan Musial makes his debut with the Cardinals on September 17 and bats .426 the rest of the season.
1942	The Cardinals clinch their fourth World Series title on October 5 with a 4–2 defeat of the Yankees.
1944	The Cardinals win another World Series title on October 9 with a 3–1 win over the St. Louis Browns in Game 6.

1946	The Cardinals take their third World Series title in five years on October 15 with a 4–3 victory over the Boston Red Sox in the seventh and deciding game.
1964	The Cardinals win their first World Series in 22 years on October 15 with a 7–5 win over the Yankees in Game 7.
1967	Another World Series championship is secured on October 12 when the Cardinals beat the Red Sox, 7–2, in another Game 7.
1968	St. Louis ace pitcher Bob Gibson sets a major league record by posting a 1.12 ERA, but the Cardinals fall to the Detroit Tigers in a seven-game World Series.
1982	The Cardinals snag their first World Series title in 15 years on October 20 with a 6–3 win over the Milwaukee Brewers in Game 7.
1998	Mark McGwire slugs his major league record 70th home run on September 27, but he later admits that he used performance-enhancing drugs.
2001	Rookie Albert Pujols makes his debut for the Cardinals and emerges as one of the top sluggers in the game.
2006	The Cardinals clinch their first World Series title in 24 years on October 27 with a 4–2 victory over the Tigers.
2011	The Cardinals defeat the Texas Rangers in the World Series for their eleventh world championship.
2013	The Cardinals win the division and the NLCS, but they fall to the Boston Red Sox in a six-game World Series.

QUICK STATS

FRANCHISE HISTORY
St. Louis Brown Stockings (1882)
St. Louis Browns (1883–98)
St. Louis Perfectos (1899)
St. Louis Cardinals (1900–)

WORLD SERIES
(wins in bold)
1926, 1928, 1930, **1931**, **1934**, **1942**, 1943, **1944**, **1946**, **1964**, **1967**, 1968, **1982**, 1985, 1987, 2004, **2006**, **2011**, 2013

NL CHAMPIONSHIP SERIES
(1969–)
1982, 1985, 1987, 1996, 2000, 2002, 2004, 2005, 2006, 2011, 2013

DIVISION CHAMPIONSHIPS
(1969–)
1982, 1985, 1987, 1996, 2000, 2002, 2004, 2005, 2006, 2009, 2011, 2012, 2013

KEY PLAYERS
(position, seasons with team)
Ken Boyer (3B; 1955–65)
Lou Brock (OF; 1964–79)
Dizzy Dean (P; 1930, 1932–37)
Frankie Frisch (2B; 1927–37)
Bob Gibson (SP; 1959–75)
Rogers Hornsby (OF; 1915–26, 1933)
Joe Medwick (OF; 1932–40, 1947–48)
Stan Musial (OF; 1941–44, 1946-63)
Albert Pujols (1B; 2001–11)
Ted Simmons (C; 1968–80)
Enos Slaughter (OF; 1938–42, 1946–53)
Ozzie Smith (SS; 1982–96)
Bill White (1B; 1959–65, 1969)

KEY MANAGERS
Whitey Herzog (1980–90): 822–728; 21–16 (postseason)
Tony La Russa (1996–2011): 1,408–1,182; 50–42 (postseason)

HOME PARKS
Sportsman's Park I (1882–92)
Robison Field (1893–1920)
Sportsman's Park IV (1920–66)
    Known as Busch Stadium (1953–66)
Busch Stadium II (1966–2005)
Busch Stadium III (2006–)

* All statistics through 2013 season

QUOTES AND ANECDOTES

Cardinals shortstop Ozzie Smith delighted St. Louis fans with his trademark cartwheel and back flip as he ran out to his position before the first and last day of the season and before big postseason games.

Bob Gibson is the Cardinals' leader in nearly every career pitching statistical category. He sits atop the team list in innings pitched (3,884 1/3), wins (251), complete games (255), shutouts (56), and strikeouts (3,117). He is more than 2,000 strikeouts ahead of Dizzy Dean, who is third in that department.

Twenty-three perfect games had been pitched in the major leagues through the 2013 season. Not one of them was hurled for or against the Cardinals. The only St. Louis pitcher to throw two no-hitters was Bob Forsch, who achieved the feat in a 5–0 win over the Philadelphia Phillies in 1978 and a 3–0 blanking of the Montreal Expos five years later.

"I can't believe it happened. I did not expect to hit another one. I've never been a home run hitter. I just tried to meet the ball. I'm not like Mark McGwire." —Cardinals third baseman Fernando Tatis after smashing two grand slams in one game at the Los Angeles Dodgers on April 23, 1999.

"The dumber a pitcher is, the better. When he gets smart and begins to experiment with a lot of different pitches, he's in trouble. All I ever had was a fastball, a curve, and a change-up and I did pretty good."—Dizzy Dean

GLOSSARY

ace

A team's best starting pitcher.

attendance

The number of fans who come to watch a team play during a particular season or game.

clinch

To officially settle something, such as a berth in the playoffs.

clubhouse

A large room where baseball players change clothes and relax before and after games.

contend

To be in the race for a championship or playoff berth.

durable

Healthy and strong.

farm system

A big-league club's teams in the minor leagues, where players are developed for the majors.

mediocre

Neither good nor bad.

pennant

A flag. In baseball, it symbolizes that a team has won its league championship.

postseason

The games in which the best teams play after the regular-season schedule has been completed.

retire

To officially end one's career.

rookie

A first-year player in the major leagues.

strike

A work stoppage by employees in protest of working conditions.

wild card

Playoff berths given to the best remaining teams that did not win their respective divisions.

FOR MORE INFORMATION

Further Reading

Feldmann, Doug. *St. Louis Cardinals Past & Present*. Osceola, WI: MVP Books, 2009.

Snyder, John. *Cardinals Journal: Year by Year and Day by Day With the St. Louis Cardinals Since 1882*. Cincinnati, OH: Clerisy Press, 2010.

Stewart, Wayne. *Stan the Man: The Life and Career of Stan Musial*. Chicago: Triumph Books, 2010.

Websites

To learn more about Inside MLB, visit **booklinks.abdopublishing.com**. These links are routinely monitored and updated to provide the most current information available.

Places to Visit

Busch Stadium
700 Clark Street
St. Louis, MO 63102
314-345-9000
mlb.mlb.com/stl/ballpark/index.jsp
This has been the Cardinals' home field since 2006. Tours are available when the Cardinals are not playing.

National Baseball Hall of Fame and Museum
25 Main Street
Cooperstown, NY 13326
888-HALL-OF-FAME
www.baseballhall.org
This hall of fame and museum highlights the greatest players and moments in the history of baseball. Dizzy Dean, Bob Gibson, Rogers Hornsby, Stan Musial, and Ozzie Smith are among the former Cardinals enshrined there.

Roger Dean Stadium
4795 University Blvd.
Jupiter, FL 33458
561-775-1818
www.rogerdeanstadium.com
Roger Dean Stadium has been the Cardinals' spring-training ballpark since 1998. The Cardinals share the stadium with the Florida Marlins.

INDEX

About the Author

Marty Gitlin is a freelance writer based in Cleveland, Ohio. He has written more than 25 educational books, including many about sports. Gitlin has won more than 45 awards during his 25 years as a writer, including first place for general excellence from the Associated Press. He lives with his wife and three children in Ohio.